Christus Natus Est

A CHRISTMAS SERVICE OF READINGS & MUSIC

Compiled by H. J. Richards with music by George Malcolm

Kevin Mayhew

We hope you enjoy *Christus Natus Est.*
Further copies are available from your local music or christian bookshop.

In case of difficulty, please contact the publisher direct:

The Sales Department
KEVIN MAYHEW LTD
Rattlesden
Bury St Edmunds
Suffolk IP30 0SZ
Phone 0449 737978   Fax 0449 737834

Please ask for our complete catalogue of outstanding Church Music.

The texts in this book may be reproduced without charge for
a single occasion with the exception of those listed below. Permission to reproduce these texts must
be made to the individual copyright owners.

Acknowledgements
The publishers wish to express their gratitude to the following for permission to use copyright material:

Faber and Faber Ltd, 3 Queen Square, London WC1N 3AU for *The Cultivation of Christmas Trees*
from *Collected Poems 1909-1962* by T. S. Eliot.

John Murray (Publishers) Ltd, 50 Albermarle Street, London W1X 4BD for *Christmas* by John Betjeman
from his *Collected Poems*.

National Christian Education Council, Robert Denholm House, Nutfield, Redhill, Surrey RH1 4HW for
Here is a cross, a sign of the love by Jan Pickard from *A Word in Season*, 1984, edited by Donald Hilton.

Ted Schmidt for Readings Number 9 and 10.

Front Cover: *Mystic Nativity* by Sandro Botticelli (1445-1510).
Reproduced by courtesy of the Trustees, The National Gallery, London.

First published in Great Britain in 1992 by

KEVIN MAYHEW LTD
Rattlesden
Bury St Edmunds
Suffolk IP30 0SZ

ISBN 0 86209 304 X

© Copyright 1992 by Kevin Mayhew Ltd.

Music setting by Tricia Oliver
Cover design by Graham Johnstone
Printed and bound in Great Britain

Contents

Foreword

This book contains eight Latin 'responsories' set to music by George Malcolm when he was Master of Music at Westminster Cathedral between 1947 and 1959. The pieces were designed as choral interludes between the nine readings at the night office of Matins which preceded the midnight Mass of Christmas. Each year their performance was eagerly awaited by both choir and congregation, the simplicity and beauty of the music claiming a special place in the memory of all who heard it.

The liturgical reforms introduced by the Second Vatican Council (1963–65) were designed to encourage more popular participation in the Prayer of the Church. Worship originally intended for monastic communities, and conducted exclusively in Latin, needed to be simplified and translated into the vernacular. In the event, the rather unwieldy service of Matins was turned into a simple office of three psalms and two readings. Responsories were no longer required, least of all in Latin.

All reforms, even those long overdue, sadly leave casualties behind: witness the sparse jewels which remain (*Abba, Amen, Alleluia, Kyrie Eleison*) to remind western Christians of their glorious Hebrew and Greek past. Lest our even more long-standing Latin heritage be similarly consigned to oblivion, these fine pieces by George Malcolm have here been incorporated into a Christmas service, introduced by a congregational hymn, and concluding with bidding prayers, a collect, and a recessional hymn. A number of readings have been included from which the celebrant may wish to make a choice as he deems appropriate. It is for the celebrant also to decide how the lighting of candles and the use of incense may enhance the celebration.

The composer, editor and publisher are aware of the importance of the Christmas season in the Church's liturgical year. They hope this book will help Christians celebrate the feast with a sense of wonder and of joy.

H. J. Richards

Introduction

The hymn *Let all mortal flesh keep silence* may be sung, or the following to any Long Metre tune, though *Conditor Alme* is especially recommended.

1. Jesus, Redeemer of all men,
   who ere created light began
   didst from the sovereign Father spring,
   His power and glory equalling!

2. The Father's light and splendour thou
   their endless hope to thee that bow;
   accept the prayers and praise today
   that through the world thy servants pay.

3. The heavens above, the rolling main
   and all that earth's wide realms contain,
   with joyous voice now loudly sing
   the glory of their newborn King.

4. And we who by thy precious blood
   from sin redeemed are marked for God,
   on this the day that saw thy birth
   sing the new song of ransomed earth.

5. All honour, praise and glory be
   O Jesus, Virgin-born, to thee;
   all glory, as is ever meet,
   to Father and to Paraclete. Amen.

FIRST RESPONSORY

1. Ho-di-e no-bis Cae-lo-rum Rex de vir-gi-ne na-sci di-gna-tus est, ut ho-mi-nem per-di-tum ad cae-le - sti-a re-gna re-vo-ca - ret.

Gau - det ex-er - ci-tus an-ge-lo - rum, qui-a

1. This day, in his goodness, the King of Heaven has been born for us of a Virgin, and brought back to the heavenly Kingdom the lost human race.

Response *The angel host rejoices, because the human race has seen its eternal salvation.*

2. Glory to God in the highest, and on earth peace to men of good will.

3. Glory be to the Father and to the Son and to the Holy Spirit.

SECOND RESPONSORY

1. This day true peace has come down to us from heaven.

Response *This day, this day the skies rain down sweetness all over the world.*

2. This day we have been set free again, paradise has been restored, and everlasting happiness promised us.

Third Responsory overleaf

1. Whom have you seen, you shepherds?
   Speak, tell us who has appeared on earth?

Response *We have seen a child, and choirs of angels singing the praises of the Lord.*

2. Tell us what you have seen, and proclaim the birth of Christ.

3. Glory be to the Father and to the Son and to the Holy Spirit.

THIRD RESPONSORY

At the end of each verse hold chord on to the first beat of the Response.

Cantor

mp

2. Di - ci - te quid - nam vi - di - stis, et an - nun - ti -

pp

Ped. 8'

dim. Repeat Response

a - te Chri - sti na - ti - vi - ta - tem.

Sopranos and Altos

pp

pp

3. Glo - ri - a Pa - tri et Fi - li -

Ped. 8'

dim. Repeat Response

o, et Spi - ri - tu - i San - cto.

FOURTH RESPONSORY

1. What a great mystery! What a wondrous sign!
That the beasts should behold the birth of their Lord, lying in a manger.

Response *Blessed is the Virgin whose womb was worthy to bear Christ the Lord.*

2. Hail Mary, full of grace, the Lord is with thee.

Response

Be - a - ta vir - go, cu - jus vi - sce - ra me - ru -

e - runt por - ta - re Do - mi - num Chri - stum.

Cantor

2. A - ve, Ma - ri - a, gra - ti - a ple - na,

Repeat Response

Do - mi - nus te - cum.

FIFTH RESPONSORY

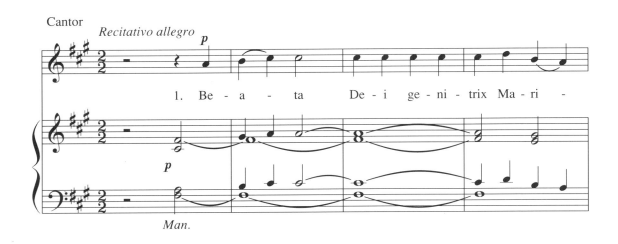

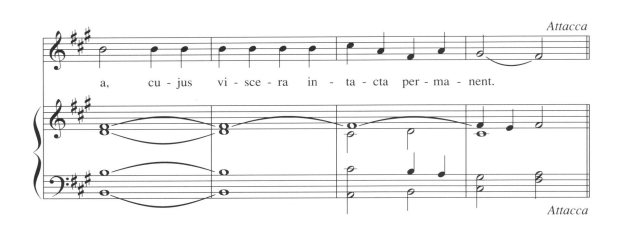

Cantor

2. Be - a - ta quae credidit, quoniam perfecta sunt o - mni -

Repeat Response

a, quae di - cta sunt e - i a Do - mi - no.

1. Blessed is Mary, the Mother of God, whose womb remains undefiled.

Response This day she has borne the Saviour of the world.

2. Blessed is she for her faith, for everything the Lord promised her has come to pass.

Sixth Responsory overleaf

1. Holy Virgin undefiled, I know not how to praise thee.

Response *For him whom the heavens cannot contain thou hast brought forth from thy womb.*

2. Blessed art thou among women, and blessed is the fruit of thy womb.

3. Glory be to the Father and to the Son and to the Holy Spirit.

SIXTH RESPONSORY

Cantor

2. Be - ne - di - cta   tu   in   mu - li - e - ri - bus,

Repeat Response

et   be - ne - di - ctus fru - ctus   ven - tris   tu - i.

Sopranos and Altos

3. Glo - ri - a   Pa - tri   et   Fi - li - o

Repeat Response

et   Spi - ri - tu - i   San   -   cto.

17

SEVENTH RESPONSORY

1. Beata viscera Mariae Vir - gi - nis quae portaverunt aeterni Pa - tris Fi - li -

Cantor
Recitativo allegro
mp

Man.

um: et beata ubera / quae la - cta - ve - runt Chri - stum Do - mi - num.

Response
Allegro
mp

Qui ho - di - e pro sa - lu - te mun - di de

de

Cantor

2. Dies sanctifi - ca - tus il - lu - xit no - bis:

Repeat Response

venite gen - tes et a - do - ra - te Do - mi - num.

1. Blessed is the womb of the Virgin Mary, which bore the Son of the eternal Father: and blessed are the breasts which gave suck to Christ the Lord.

Response *Who this day, in his goodness, to save the world, was born of a Virgin.*

2. The blessed day has dawned on us: come, you nations, and worship the Lord.

EIGHTH RESPONSORY

1. The Word was made flesh and dwelt amongst us.

Response   *And we have seen his glory, the glory he has from the Father as his only Son, full of grace and truth.*

2. All things were made through him, and without him nothing was made.

3. Glory be to the Father and to the Son and to the Holy Spirit.

glo - ri - am qua-si u - ni - ge - ni - ti a Pa - tre,

ple - num gra - ti-ae et ve - ri - ta - tis.

2. O - mni - a per i - psum fa - cta sunt:

Repeat Response

et si - ne i - pso fa - ctum est ni - hil.

Lento

3. Glo - ri - a Pa - tri et Fi - li - o:

Repeat Response

et Spi - ri - tu - i San - cto.

A Selection of Readings

1

Time was when Galilee was humbled by invaders:
the time will come when its glory will be restored.
A people that dwelt in darkness will see a great light:
on those who were overshadowed by death, light will shine again.

You have given new heart to this people, O God,
and they rejoice as people do at harvest time,
as victors do when they share the spoils:
for you have broken the yoke that crushed them
and the tyrant's rod that oppressed them,
as you did when Gideon overthrew the Midianites.
All the heavy army-boots and bloodstained uniforms
will now feed the flames and be burnt.

For a child has been born for us, a son given to us,
and he shall be robed in the royal purple,
and these titles conferred on him:
'Wonderful Counsellor, Mighty God,
Eternal Father, Prince of Peace.'

ISAIAH 9:1-6 *Traditional reading for 1st Nocturn*

2

Take comfort, my people, take comfort –
it is the voice of your God –
bid Jerusalem be of good heart,
and tell her she has completed her prison sentence
and paid her penalty in full.

Listen! A voice is crying out:
make a road through the wilderness for the Lord,
cut a highway across the desert for our God;
fill in the valleys and level the hills,
straighten the bends and smooth the ground,
so that the glory of the Lord may be seen by all,
and all people behold what the Lord has decreed.

All humanity is grass, lasting no longer than wild flowers:
the grass withers and flowers fade
as soon as the Lord breathes on them;
but the word of our God stands for ever.

ISAIAH 40:1-8 *Traditional reading for 1st Nocturn*

3

My dear brothers and sisters:
This is the day our Saviour was born: what a joy for us!
We must have no sadness today
when Life has been born,
and our fear of death taken away,
and the joy of eternity promised to us.

And you must all rejoice,
because it is all of us that our Lord has come to liberate.
If you are a saint, rejoice: your reward is before you.
If you are a sinner, rejoice: pardon is being offered you.
If you are an outsider, take heart: life is within your grasp.
In this fullness of time
God has sent his Son to share our human nature
and win the fight we humans had lost.

My dear brothers and sisters:
Let us give thanks to God the Father,
through his Son, in the Holy Spirit,
who, through the greatness of his love,
has taken pity on us, dead in our sinfulness,
and given us new life in Christ.

Do you realise what special people you Christians are?
You have been raised on to God's own level,
and given a share in God's own nature.
How can you think of going back
to the sinful life you lived beforehand?
Think of the Head, and think of the Body
of which you have become a member.
Remember that you have been rescued out of the darkness,
and found a place in the light, the Kingdom of God.

St Leo the Great 440-461 *Traditional reading for 2nd Nocturn*

4

There has never been a time
when God has not told people that he loves them.
Right from the beginning,
and through all the ages,
that is what he has told all people everywhere.

But not all people have understood
what God was telling them,
even when God was saying, in so many words:
Come and be members of my family.

So this Word of God became human

and lived a human life like ours,
so that we could touch and feel what God was telling us.
The Word was made flesh and dwelt amongst us.
In him we see the God who can't be seen.
In him we see that God loves us.

JOHN 1:1—18 *Traditional reading for 3rd Nocturn*

5

The Almighty himself, Creator of the universe,
the God whom no eye can discern,
has sent down from heaven his very own Truth, his holy Word,
to be planted in the heart of the human race.

To do this, one might have imagined he would send
some servant, some angel, some prince.
But no. He has sent the very Artificer and Constructor
  of the universe,
through whom the heavens were made,
and the seas set within their bounds,
whose word is obeyed by the very elements of creation,
who assigns the sun the limits of its course by day,
and commands the moon to unveil its beams by night,
and orders the obedient stars to circle the heavens.
He is the Ordainer, Disposer and Ruler of all things,
of all that is in heaven and earth,
of the seas and all that they contain
of fire, and air, and the deep,
of all that is above and below and in between.
Such is the Messenger God has sent to the human race.

One might have imagined that his coming
would be in power, terror and awesomeness.
But no. His coming was in gentleness and humility.
God sent him as a king might send his own son,
and he came among us as a fellow human being.
For God would save us by persuasion, not by compulsion,
(there is no compulsion to be found in God)
and he sent him not to judge us, but out of love.

The Epistle to Diognetus, 2nd cent.

6

The world is charged with the grandeur of God.
It will flame out, like shining from shook foil;
it gathers to a greatness, like the ooze of oil
crushed. Why do men then now not reck his rod?
Generations have trod, have trod, have trod;
and all is seared with trade; bleared, smeared with toil;

and wears man's smudge and shares man's smell:
the soil is bare now, nor can foot feel, being shod.

And for all this, nature is never spent;
there lives the dearest freshness deep down things;
and though the last lights off the black West went,
morning, at the brown brink eastward, springs –
because the Holy Ghost over the bent
world broods with warm breast and with ah! bright wings.

GERARD MANLEY HOPKINS 1844-1889

7 There are several attitudes towards Christmas,
Some of which we may disregard:
The social, the torpid, the patently commercial,
The rowdy (the pubs being open till midnight),
And the childish — which is not that of the child
For whom the candle is a star, and the gilded angel
Spreading its wings at the summit of the tree
Is not only a decoration, but an angel.
The child wonders at the Christmas Tree:
Let him continue in the spirit of wonder
At the Feast as an event, not accepted as a pretext;
So that the glittering rapture, the amazement
Of the first-remembered Christmas Tree,
So that the surprises, delight in new possessions
(Each one with its peculiar and exciting smell),
The expectation of the goose or turkey
And the expected awe on its appearance,
So that the reverence and the gaiety
May not be forgotten in later experience,
In the bored habituation, the fatigue, the tedium,
The awareness of death, the consciousness of failure,
Or in the piety of the convert
Which may be tainted with a self-conceit
Displeasing to God and disrespectful to the children
(And here I remember also with gratitude
St. Lucy, her carol, and her crown of fire):
So that before the end, the eightieth Christmas
(By "eightieth" meaning whichever is the last)
The accumulated memories of annual emotion
May be concentrated into a great joy
Which shall also be a great fear, as on the occasion
When fear came upon every soul:
Because the beginning shall remind us of the end
And the first coming of the second coming.

T. S. ELIOT 1888-1965   *The Cultivation of Christmas Trees*

8

And is it true? And is it true,
this most tremendous tale of all,
seen in a stained-glass window's hue,
a Baby in an ox's stall?
The Maker of the stars and sea
become a child on earth for me?

And is it true? For if it is,
no loving fingers tying strings
around those tissued fripperies,
the sweet and silly Christmas things
bath salts and inexpensive scent,
and hideous tie so kindly meant,

No love that in a family dwells,
no carolling in frosty air,
nor all the steeple-shaking bells
can with this single truth compare –
that God was man in Palestine
and lives today in Bread and Wine.

J. BETJEMAN, 1906-1984. *Christmas.*

9

You will find a baby wrapped in swaddling clothes (Luke 2:12)
Such news was and always will be
incomprehensible.
The glory of God is a baby totally naked.
The longed for light that breaks
the darkness
is a child's translucent skin.
The hopeful voice that will summon the dead
comes not from the barracks, the Capitol or the Temple.
It is an infant's wail deep in a cave.
It is a total surprise,
absolute shock and sheer grace.
The Mystery's name and God's claim is
vulnerability.
The only birth announcement
proclaimed in an empty field
to shepherds on the margins of life
was 'Glory to God in the highest heaven'.
Maranatha, O naked baby.

TED SCHMIDT 1985

10

We wait for something, someone
to light our twentieth century night of death
to redeem the seventy-eight million who died
to keep the world a safer place for democracy
(and profit and control).

We wait for the birth of the one
who will stay the final anointing of cinder and ash
who will make it all new
transform our lives
heal our necrophilia.

We can no longer abide the official optimism
of those who invoke the bigger pie.
There are no tears here, nothing of solidarity or hope
no understanding of the view from the edge.
There is no realisation that the Kingdom-bringer
waits in the virgin womb, ripe
to burst forth with liberty for the captives.
It is rumoured that thrones will be upended
and every Caesar stands on a banana skin.
Christos, the Holy One of God, will never
bless the silos, wear the military tunic
or sanctify the Empire.

He will offer a new heaven and a new earth
and to toast his Christmas arrival
you must also dance at his Friday coronation.

Emmanuel, come warm our global stable
with Spirit fire.

TED SCHMIDT 1988

11

Here is our cross, a sign of the love
in the life of a man
who shows us the way that God loves.

This is the woman
who said 'Yes' to God
and carried the baby
who grew to a man
and showed us the way
that God loves.

Here's an old man, who worked with his hands
and hammered the wood,

who cared for the woman
who carried the baby
who grew to a man
who showed us the way that God loves.

This is the busy landlord in Bethlehem town
who lent them a shed with hay for a bed
for the old man who worked with his hands
and cared for the woman
who carried the baby
who grew to a man
who showed us the way that God loves.

These are the shepherds out in all weathers
who heard the Good News and came running down
to Bethlehem town
to find in the shed the landlord had lent
just an old man who worked with his hands
and cared for the woman
who carried her baby
who grew to a man
and showed us the way that God loves.

These are poor people
all sad and afraid
and ill and alone
who saw the Good News
in the life of the man
who showed us the way that God loves.

These are the children
who wanted to play −
more joyful than grownups who chased them away −
and found they belonged
very close to the man
who showed us the way that God loves.

You are the people
to share the Good News
of the small children who came to belong
and the poor people who found they were free
and the rough shepherds who glorified God
and all busy people who find a small space
for the old man who worked with his hands
and the young woman who said 'Yes' to God
and that little boy who grew to a man

and carried a cross
and shows us the way that God loves.

JAN PICKARD

12

Tonight the wind gnaws
with teeth of glass,
the jackdaw shivers
in caged branches of iron,
the stars have talons.

There is hunger in the mouth
of vole and badger,
silver agonies of breath
in the nostril of the fox,
ice on the rabbit's paw.

Tonight has no moon,
no food for the pilgrim.
The fruit tree is bare,
the rose bush a thorn,
and the ground bitter with stones.

But the mole sleeps, and the hedgehog
lies curled in a womb of leaves.
The bean and the wheatseed
hug their germs in the earth,
and the stream moves under the ice.

Tonight there is no moon —
but a new star opens
like a silver trumpet over the dead.
Tonight in a nest of ruins
the blessed babe is laid.

And the fir tree warms to a bloom of candles,
the child lights his lantern,
stares at his tinselled toy,
our hearts and hearths
smoulder with live ashes.

In the blood of our grief
the cold earth is suckled;
in our agony the womb
convulses its seed;
in the cry of anguish
the child's first breath is born.

Source unknown   *Laurie Lee*

A Selection of Bidding Prayers

1

Lord God, we commend to you our whole world,
all countries, races, nations and peoples,
both young and old, rich and poor.
Lord in your mercy. **Hear our prayer.**

2

We call to mind all those who have now died
but who have bequeathed this world to us:
our parents and ancestors,
all those who have made us what we are,
and given us our language to speak,
and our country to live in.
Lord in your mercy. **Hear our prayer.**

3

We pray for our children and our children's children,
and for all who will be born after us,
that we do not give them stones instead of bread,
that we do not bequeath war to them,
but freedom, happiness and peace.
Lord in your mercy. **Hear our prayer.**

4

We remember your command to us
to love those whom we dislike, and who dislike us,
our enemies and those whom we avoid,
and so we pray for them too.
But above all we pray for those
who are closest to us in friendship and love,
and who make this world meaningful for us.
Lord in you mercy. **Hear our prayer.**

5

Lord Jesus Christ, poorest of the poor,
born in a borrowed stable
and buried in a borrowed tomb,
we bring before you all those who, like you,
have nowhere to lay their head:
the war refugees exiled from their homes,
migrants searching for a place to live,
the victims of earthquakes, floods and disasters,
and the countless, countless homeless in our own land.
Help us, who live securely and in peace,
to show compassion for our brothers and sisters,
and give their lives a new beginning and hope.
Lord in your mercy. **Hear our prayer.**

A Selection of Collects

1 Lord Jesus Christ,
although you were rich,
you became poor for our sake,
so that we could become rich
through your poverty.
Fill us with that same spirit of generosity
so that we can learn how to enrich the poor,
and how to be enriched by their poverty.

2 Almighty God, Father and Saviour,
your kindness overwhelms us,
your great love for the human race.
You have not saved us because we deserved it,
but simply out of your faithful love for us.
Glory be to you, our God,
who lives and reigns for ever and ever. Amen.

3 Almighty God and Father,
we have come together to give you thanks
for the birth of your Son Jesus,
whose whole life
was an embodiment of you
and of all your promises.
We ask you to help us now
to become *his* embodiment,
so that on seeing us
people will again see him,
and in seeing him, find you,
who lives and reigns for ever and ever. Amen.

Recessional

The hymn *Hark the herald angels sing* may be sung.